# AI Investing For Gen Z:

## How Artificial Intelligence Can

## Supercharge Your Savings

**Jeffery Long**

**Copyright © 2024 by Jeffery Long**

All rights reserved. No part of this book may be reproduced or transmitted in any form or by any means, electronic or mechanical, including photocopying, recording, or by any information storage and retrieval system, without permission in writing from the publisher.

Disclaimer: The information contained in this book is for educational and informational purposes only. The author and publisher are not liable for any losses or damages incurred as a result of the use of this information.

Printed in the United States of America

First Edition

# Chapter 1:

## The Future of Finance is Here

Okay, Gen Z, let's have a real, no-BS conversation. I know the word "finance" might make you want to roll your eyes so hard they get stuck in the back of your head. It conjures up images of stuffy suits, boring spreadsheets, and lectures from your parents that sound like a foreign language.

But hold up! This isn't your grandma's finance class. We're talking about something way more exciting: taking control of your financial destiny in a world where technology is rewriting the rules of the game.

**You're the Digital Natives, the TikTok Titans, the Meme Masters**

Think about it. You were practically born with a smartphone in your hand. You're the generation that grew up with social media, streaming services, and the internet as your playground. You're used to instant gratification, constant connection, and the ability to access information with a single swipe.

So, why should managing your money be any different? Why should it be stuck in the Stone Age when the rest of your life is moving at warp speed?

The answer is simple: It shouldn't! And that's where AI investing comes in. It's like having a financial superhero by your side, a digital sidekick that's smarter, faster, and more efficient than any human advisor. It's about harnessing the power of technology to make your money work for you, not the other way around.

**Gen Z: The Financial Underdogs with a Secret Weapon**

Let's be honest, your generation has been dealt a bit of a raw deal. Student loan debt is piled high, the cost of living is through the roof, and finding a decent-paying job feels like winning the lottery. It's enough to make anyone want to throw in the towel and binge-watch their favorite show for the fifth time.

But here's the thing: You're also the most adaptable, tech-savvy generation in history. You're not afraid to question the old ways of doing things and blaze your own trail. You're creative, resourceful, and you know how to hustle. And guess what?That gives you a massive advantage when it comes to building wealth.

AI investing is the ultimate equalizer, the secret weapon that can level the playing field and give you the same opportunities as the Wall Street bigwigs. With AI, you can tap into the power of data and technology to make informed investment decisions, even if you're starting with just a few bucks in your pocket. It's like having a team of financial experts working for you around the clock, analyzing market trends, crunching numbers and uncovering hidden opportunities - all while you're catching up on the latest memes.

**The Time to Act is Now: Plant Your Money Tree Today**

I know, I know... you're young. You've got your whole life ahead of you. Why worry about money now?

Well, here's the deal: the earlier you start investing, the more time your money has to grow. It's like planting a tree. The sooner you plant it, the more time it has to soak up the sun, dig its roots deep, and reach for the sky.

Imagine this: You invest just $100 a month, starting at age 20. Let's say you earn an average annual return of 7% (which is totally doable in the long run). By the time you hit retirement age, you could have over a million dollars! That's the mind-blowing power of compound interest, and AI can help you harness it like a pro.

But it's not just about retirement, it's about creating a life where you're not constantly stressed about money. Imagine being able to travel the world, start your own business, or simply have the freedom to pursue your passions without worrying about paying the bills. That's the kind of future AI investing can help you build.

**Your Financial Future Awaits**

So, are you ready to ditch the financial stress and embrace a future where you're in control? Are you ready to unleash the power of AI investing and supercharge your savings? Because let's face it, financial freedom isn't just about having a fat bank account. It's about having the power to design your life on your terms. It's about waking up every day excited about the possibilities, not dreading the bills piling up on your desk.

Think about it - what would it feel like to have the means to travel the world, pursue your passions without worrying about the paycheck, or simply have the peace of mind that comes with knowing you're financially secure? That's the kind of future we're talking about here.

This book is your roadmap to that future. It's not just about throwing around fancy financial terms or making you feel overwhelmed with complicated charts and graphs. We're going to dive deep into the world of AI investing, but we're going to do it in a way that's fun, relatable, and easy to understand.

We'll break down complex concepts into bite-sized pieces, share real-world examples of how other young people are using AI to crush their financial goals, and give you actionable steps you can take today to start building your financial empire. No more feeling lost or confused about money matters. No more relying on outdated advice or hoping for the best.

This is about taking charge, being proactive, and using the tools of the 21st century to create the life you deserve. It's about understanding that financial literacy isn't just for the rich or the "adults" - it's for anyone who wants to live a life of freedom, abundance, and possibility.

So get ready to high-five your future self, because things are about to get exciting! We're about to embark on a journey that will not only transform your relationship with money but also empower you to create a future that's brighter, bolder, and more fulfilling than you ever imagined. Let's do this!

Chapter 2:

**Demystifying AI: Your New Financial Sidekick**

Okay, Gen Z, let's get one thing straight: AI isn't just some futuristic sci-fi concept reserved for brainiacs in lab coats. It's already here, woven into the fabric of our everyday lives, and it's about to revolutionize the way you handle your finances.But before we unleash the power of AI on your savings goals, let's peel back the curtain and demystify this whole AI thing.

Think of AI as your trusty financial sidekick, always ready to lend a helping hand, like a super-smart, data-crunching Robin to your Batman. It's like having a personal financial advisor who's read every book, analyzed every market trend, and crunched every number imaginable - all without charging you an arm and a leg!

## AI: The Brainpower Behind the Scenes

At its core, AI is all about teaching machines to think and learn like humans – minus the coffee breaks and procrastination, of course! We feed them massive amounts of data, and they use clever algorithms to analyze patterns, make predictions, and even come up with creative solutions. It's like having a financial guru who's constantly learning and adapting, always one step ahead of the market, and never gets tired or needs a vacation.

But don't worry, AI isn't here to steal your job or take over the world (at least not yet!). It's here to make your life easier and help you make smarter decisions. Think of it as a tool, just like your smartphone or your laptop. It's all about how you use it. You're still the captain of your financial ship; AI is just your trusty navigator, helping you chart the best course.

Now, let's geek out for a minute and take a peek under the hood of AI. It's where the real magic happens!

**Machine Learning:** Picture this - you're trying to teach a computer to recognize cats in photos. You show it thousands of pictures of cats, and it starts to identify patterns: pointy ears, whiskers, furry tails. That's machine learning in a nutshell! It's like giving a computer a crash course in pattern recognition. It sifts through mountains of data, spots trends, and makes predictions based on what it's learned. In the world of investing, machine learning algorithms can analyze historical stock prices, economic indicators, and even news headlines to predict future market movements. It's like having a crystal ball, but instead of relying on vague prophecies, it's based on cold, hard data.

**Neural Networks:** These bad boys are inspired by the human brain itself. They're complex systems of interconnected nodes that process information in a way that mimics our own thought processes. This allows AI to tackle more complex tasks, like understanding natural language (think Siri or Alexa) or recognizing faces in photos.In finance, neural networks can be used to analyze complex market trends, identify potential risks, and even create personalized investment strategies based on your individual goals and preferences. It's like having a team of financial experts working tirelessly behind the scenes, crunching numbers and uncovering hidden opportunities.

**Natural Language Processing (NLP)**: Ever chatted with a chatbot online or asked your voice assistant to play your favorite song? That's NLP in action! It's the magic that lets AI understand and respond to human language. In the world of investing, NLP can be used to analyze news articles, social media sentiment, and even company earnings calls to gauge market sentiment and make informed investment decisions. It's like having a team of analysts scouring the internet 24/7, keeping you up-to-date on the latest market trends.

So, there you have it – a glimpse into the inner workings of AI. It's not just about robots and self-driving cars; it's about harnessing the power of data and technology to make your life easier and your financial decisions smarter.

In the next section, we'll explore some real-world examples of how AI is already transforming the finance industry and how you can leverage these tools to supercharge your savings. Get ready to be amazed!

## AI in Finance: Real-World Examples

So, how exactly is artificial intelligence transforming the finance landscape in truly significant and impactful ways? Let's explore several concrete real-world examples that are already making a substantial difference and creating considerable waves throughout the industry:

- **Robo-advisors:** These AI-powered platforms create personalized investment portfolios based on your goals, risk tolerance, and time horizon. They take the emotion out of investing, making decisions based on data and algorithms rather than gut feelings. Plus, they're available 24/7, so you can check in on your investments whenever you want, even if it's 3 AM and you can't sleep.
- **Fraud detection:** AI algorithms can analyze millions of transactions in real-time, flagging suspicious activity and preventing fraud

before it happens. This means your hard-earned money is safer than ever before. It's like having a digital bodyguard watching over your bank account.

- **Credit scoring:** AI is being used to develop more accurate and inclusive credit scoring models. This means that even if you're just starting out and don't have a long credit history, AI can take a more holistic look at your financial behavior and give you a fair shot at getting a loan or credit card.

- **Customer service chatbots:** Remember those frustrating phone calls where you're put on hold for hours, listening to elevator music? AI-powered chatbots are changing that. They can provide instant answers to your questions and help you resolve issues quickly, 24/7. It's like having a customer service rep in your pocket, ready to help whenever you need it.

- **Algorithmic Trading:** Picture this: Wall Street traders frantically shouting buy and sell orders on the trading floor. Now, replace those traders with super-fast computers running complex algorithms. That's algorithmic trading in action, where AI-powered systems execute trades at mind-boggling speeds, taking advantage of tiny market fluctuations that humans might miss. It's like having a team of financial ninjas working tirelessly to maximize your returns.

- **Risk Assessment and Management:** AI can analyze massive amounts of data to assess the risk associated with different investments, helping you make more informed decisions and avoid potential pitfalls. It's like having a crystal ball that can predict the future (well, sort of). This means you can invest with more confidence, knowing that AI is helping you manage your risk.

- **Personalized Financial Advice:** AI can crunch your personal financial data to offer tailored advice on everything from budgeting to saving to investing. It's like having a financial advisor in your pocket, available 24/7. No more stuffy boardrooms or intimidating financial jargon – just clear, personalized advice that makes sense for *you*.

## Busting the AI Myths: Let's Clear The Air

Okay, let's tackle some of the AI myths that might be swirling around in your head, causing a bit of hesitation. It's time to set the record straight and bust these misconceptions wide open!

### Myth #1: AI is only for tech geniuses.

*Pffft!* That's like saying you need a PhD in rocket science to use a smartphone. Nope! AI-powered tools are designed with *you* in mind. They're user-friendly, intuitive, and often as easy to navigate as your favorite social media app. You don't need to be a coding whiz or a mathlete to benefit from AI. In fact, many AI investing platforms are specifically designed for beginners, with simple interfaces and clear explanations. So, don't let a little fear of technology hold you back from taking control of your financial future!

### Myth #2: AI will replace human financial advisors.

Hold your horses! While AI can certainly automate many tasks and crunch numbers faster than any human, it can't replace the good ol' human touch. Think of it this way: AI is like a super-smart calculator, but a financial advisor is like a wise mentor. They can provide personalized guidance, help you navigate complex financial situations, and offer emotional support when the market gets a little bumpy.

**Myth #3: AI is too expensive.**

Let's shatter this myth right now! You don't need a trust fund or a six-figure salary to access the power of AI. In fact, many AI-powered investment platforms offer low fees or even *free* access. That's right, you can start investing with AI without breaking the bank. It's like having a personal financial advisor on a budget – who wouldn't want that?

So, instead of seeing AI as a threat, see it as a powerful tool that *enhances* the work of human advisors. It's like having a financial dream team, with AI handling the data and analysis, and your advisor providing the strategic guidance and emotional support you need to succeed.

**AI: Your Financial Wingman**

The bottom line is this: AI isn't some far-off, futuristic concept – it's your financial wingman, ready to help you navigate the exciting, sometimes overwhelming, world of money. Think of it as your personal financial coach, cheerleader, and confidante all rolled into one. It's like having a money-savvy bestie who's always got your back, helping you make smarter choices, reach your goals faster, and build a future where financial stress is a thing of the past.

So, don't be afraid to embrace the power of AI. It's time to ditch the outdated notion that finance is boring or complicated.With AI by your side, you're not just managing money; you're building a life where you're in control, confident, and empowered to achieve your wildest dreams.

# Chapter 3:

## Building Your Financial Foundation

Okay, Gen Z, let's get down to business. We've talked about the awesome potential of AI investing, and now it's time to roll up our sleeves and start building the foundation of your financial empire.

Think of this chapter as your financial boot camp. We're going to cover the basics of budgeting, saving, and investing, but we're going to do it with a Gen Z twist. No boring spreadsheets or dusty textbooks here!

## Budgeting in the Digital Age: It's Not Your Grandma's Budget

Let's face it: budgeting can sound about as exciting as watching paint dry. But in the age of smartphones and apps, budgeting has gotten a serious makeover. It's time to ditch the old-school pen-and-paper method and embrace the power of technology.

There are tons of amazing budgeting apps out there that can help you track your spending, set financial goals, and even automate your savings. It's like having a personal finance assistant in your pocket, reminding you to stay on track and celebrate your wins.

**Here's a quick step-by-step guide to get you started:**

1. **Track your income and expenses:** Start by listing all your sources of income (part-time job, allowance, side hustle, etc.) and all your expenses (rent, food, transportation, entertainment, etc.). Be honest with yourself, even if it's a little scary to see where your money is going.

2. **Set realistic goals:** What do you want to achieve with your money? Do you want to save for a down payment on a car? Pay off student loans? Travel the world? Once you know your goals, you can create a budget that works for you.

3. **Automate your savings:** The easiest way to save money is to make it automatic. Set up a recurring transfer from your checking account to your savings account each month. You won't even miss the money, and it'll add up faster than you think.

4. **Use budgeting apps:** There are tons of great budgeting apps out there

that can help you track your spending, categorize your expenses, and even give you personalized insights into your financial habits. Find one that you love and use it religiously!

**The Power of Compound Interest: Your Money's Secret Superpower**

Now, let's talk about something that's way cooler than any magic trick you'll ever see: compound interest. It's like your money's secret superpower, the financial equivalent of a snowball rolling downhill, gathering more and more snow (or in this case, money) as it goes. It's the ultimate "set it and forget it" strategy that can turn even small investments into a serious stack of cash over time.

Think of it like this: you invest $100 today. Let's say it earns a solid 10% return (which, by the way, is totally achievable in the stock market over the long term). Next year, you're not just looking at your original $100; you've got a cool $110.But here's where the magic happens: the following year, you earn another 10% return, not just on your original $100, but on the entire $110. So now, you're sitting pretty with $121. And the year after that? Another 10% on $121, and so on. It's like your money is having a growth spurt on steroids!

The earlier you start saving and investing, the more time this magical compounding has to work its wonders. It's like planting a money tree – the sooner you plant it, the bigger and more fruitful it will become. Imagine two friends, let's call them Early

Bird and Late Bloomer. Early Bird starts investing $100 a month at age 20, while Late Bloomer waits until 30 to start. Assuming they both earn a 7% annual return, by the time they reach 65, Early Bird will have a whopping $386,968, while Late Bloomer will only have $149,745. That's the difference a decade can make!

So, what's the takeaway here? Don't wait! Even if you can only spare a few bucks each week, start investing now. Let compound interest be your financial fairy godmother, turning your small investments into a sparkling future. Remember, time is your greatest asset when it comes to building wealth, so don't let it slip away.

**Actionable Tip:**

Alright, let's turn this knowledge into action! Time to put your money where your dreams are. Don't get bogged down by thinking you need a massive chunk of change to start investing. Nope! We're starting small, but mighty.

### Step 1: Open a High-Yield Savings Account

Think of this as your money's cozy little nest egg. It's a safe place to park your cash while it earns a bit of interest. Look for online banks or credit unions that offer high-yield savings accounts. These bad boys often have interest rates that are way better than traditional brick-and-mortar banks.

### Step 2: Set Up Automatic Transfers

This is where the magic happens. Set up an automatic transfer from your checking account to your savings account every week or month. Even if it's just $20 a week (that's like skipping two fancy coffees!), it adds up over time. Treat this transfer like any other bill – it's non-negotiable!

**Step 4: Celebrate Your Wins!**

Every time you make a deposit, give yourself a high-five! You're taking control of your financial future, and that's something to be proud of. Remember, consistency is key. Even small contributions, made regularly, can lead to big results thanks to the magic of compound interest.

So, what are you waiting for? Go open that savings account, set up those automatic transfers, and start watching your money grow. You've got this!

**Understanding Investment Options: Stocks, Bonds, and Beyond**

Now that you're a budgeting pro and understand the power of compound interest, it's time to explore the exciting world of investments. But before you start throwing your money at random stocks, let's take a moment to understand the different options available.

**Stocks: Own a Piece of the Pie**

Think of stocks like owning a tiny slice of your favorite company. When you buy a stock, you're essentially buying a small piece of ownership in that company. If the company does well, the value of your stock goes up, and you make money - cha-ching! But if the company struggles, the value of your stock goes down, and you might lose some money. It's a bit of a rollercoaster ride, but that's where the potential for big gains comes in.

**Real-World Example:**

Imagine you're obsessed with a new tech company that's developing self-driving cars. You believe in their vision and think they're going to be the next big thing. You buy some of their stock. A few years later, their cars are everywhere, and the company's value has skyrocketed. Your initial investment is now worth way more than you paid for it!

**Bonds: Lend a Hand, Get Paid Back**

Bonds are like being the bank, but way cooler. You're essentially lending money to a company or government. In exchange for your loan, they promise to pay you back with interest over a set period. It's a less risky way to invest because you know exactly what you're getting back, and when. But, the trade-off is that the returns are usually lower than with stocks.

**Real-World Example:**

Let's say you want to invest in something safe and predictable. You buy a bond from the U.S. government. They promise to pay you back in 10 years, plus a little bit of interest each year. It's not going to make you rich overnight, but it's a reliable way to grow your money slowly and steadily. You could also buy bonds from companies like Apple or

Coca-Cola - they're generally considered less risky than smaller, newer companies.

**ETFs (Exchange-Traded Funds): Diversify and Conquer**

ETFs are like a pre-made investment mix tape, curated by experts. They're baskets of stocks or bonds that offer instant diversification, meaning you're spreading your risk across multiple investments. It's like not putting all your eggs in one basket – if one investment goes south, you've got others to cushion the blow. ETFs are a great way to get started with investing, especially if you're not ready to pick individual stocks or bonds.

**Real-World Example:**

You're interested in investing in tech companies, but you don't want to bet on just one. You buy an ETF that tracks the performance of the top tech companies in the market, like the QQQ. Now, you're invested in a whole bunch of companies, so even if one stumbles, your overall investment is less likely to take a major hit.

**Mutual Funds: Let the Pros Handle It**

Mutual funds are similar to ETFs, but they're like having a personal chef create your investment mix tape. They pool money from many investors to invest in a diversified portfolio of stocks, bonds, or other assets. The fund is managed by a professional fund manager who makes the investment decisions for you. It's a hands-off approach, but it usually comes with higher fees than ETFs.

**Real-World Example:**

You're busy with school, work, and your social life, and you don't have the time or expertise to pick individual investments. You invest in a mutual fund that focuses on sustainable energy companies, like the Fidelity Renewable Energy Fund. The fund manager does all the research and makes the investment decisions, so you can sit back and relax (while hopefully watching your money grow).

## Real Estate: Build Your Brick-and-Mortar Empire

Real estate investing is like playing Monopoly in real life. You buy properties, rent them out, and watch your income (and hopefully property value) grow over time. It can be a great way to build long-term wealth, but it also requires a significant upfront investment and ongoing management.

**Real-World Example:**

You've saved up a chunk of change and you're ready to take the plunge into real estate. You buy a small apartment building and rent out the units. You're now a landlord, collecting rent checks each month and building equity in your property. It's a lot of responsibility, but it can also be very rewarding. Or, you might consider investing in a Real Estate Investment Trust (REIT), which allows you to invest in real estate without actually owning property.

## Cryptocurrency: The Wild West of Investing

Cryptocurrency is like the digital gold rush of the 21st century. It's a digital or virtual currency that uses cryptography for security. It's decentralized, meaning it's not controlled by any government or financial institution. Cryptocurrency is a highly volatile and speculative investment. Its value can skyrocket one day and plummet the next. But it has also seen tremendous growth in recent years, and some people believe it's the future of money.

**Real-World Example:**

You're intrigued by the potential of cryptocurrency and decide to invest a small amount in Bitcoin or Ethereum. You watch the price fluctuate wildly, sometimes feeling like you're on top of the world, and other times wanting to pull your hair out. It's a high-risk, high-reward game, but you're in it for the long haul.

**The Key is to Choose Wisely**

Remember, there's no one-size-fits-all approach to investing. The key is to choose investments that align with your financial goals, risk tolerance, and time horizon. Don't be afraid to ask questions, do your research, and seek advice from trusted sources before you invest your hard-earned money.

**Worksheet:**

- Take some time to research different investment options and make a list of those that interest you. Consider their potential returns, risks, and fees.

- Think about your financial goals and risk tolerance. Are you looking for long-term growth or short-term gains? Are you comfortable with some level of risk, or do you prefer safer investments?

Remember, investing is a marathon, not a sprint. It's about making informed decisions, staying disciplined, and letting your money grow over time. In the next chapter, we'll explore how AI can help you navigate the world of investments and make smarter choices.

# Chapter 4:

## The AI Advantage: How to Outsmart the Market

Alright, my Gen Z friends, buckle up because we're about to enter the fast lane of investing! In this chapter, we're going to unleash the full power of AI and show you how to outsmart the market like a boss. Forget relying on gut feelings or outdated advice from your grandpa – we're talking about data-driven decisions, personalized strategies, and a whole new level of financial confidence.

## AI: Your Personal Market Analyst

Remember those sci-fi movies where computers predict the future with mind-blowing accuracy? Think Minority Report or Back to the Future II. Well, we're not quite at the flying cars and hoverboards stage yet (although, wouldn't that be cool?), but when it comes to the stock market, AI is getting pretty darn close to having a crystal ball.

Think of it this way: traditionally, a market analyst is like a financial detective, spending countless hours poring over company reports, economic data, and news articles, trying to piece together the clues and predict where the market is headed. It's a bit like Sherlock Holmes, but instead of solving crimes, they're solving the mystery of which stocks are going to soar and which ones are going to tank.

Now, imagine that Sherlock Holmes had a supercomputer for a brain, capable of analyzing mountains of data in the blink of an eye. That's what AI brings to the table. AI algorithms are like financial detectives on steroids, constantly scouring massive amounts of data – everything from historical stock prices and economic indicators to news articles, social media sentiment, and even satellite images of shipping containers leaving ports. They can spot patterns and trends that even the most seasoned human analyst might miss, giving you a serious edge in the investing game.

Let's break it down even further. Imagine you're trying to pick the winning team in a basketball game. You could go with your gut feeling – maybe you're a die-hard fan of one team, or you just have a hunch. Or, you could listen to some sports commentators and see what they have to say. But let's be honest, those approaches are about as reliable as a Magic 8 Ball.

Now, imagine you had access to every player's stats, every team's past performance, the coaches' game plans, even the weather conditions on game day. Armed with that kind of information, you'd be able to make a much more informed decision, right?

That's exactly what AI does for investing. It takes the guesswork out of the equation and gives you the data you need to make smart, strategic decisions. It's like having a team of financial experts working around the clock, analyzing every bit of information available and presenting you with the most promising investment opportunities.

So, instead of relying on luck or gut feelings, you can harness the power of AI to make informed choices that align with your financial goals. It's like having a cheat code for the stock market, but instead of getting you banned, it's helping you build a brighter financial future.

**Benefits of AI-Powered Investment Platforms**

Now, let's talk about the tools that put this AI magic at your fingertips. There are tons of amazing AI-powered investment platforms out there, designed specifically for people like you – young, ambitious, and ready to take control of their financial future.

**These platforms offer a range of benefits that can supercharge your savings:**

- **Personalized Portfolios:** Forget one-size-fits-all investment strategies. AI platforms analyze your financial goals, risk tolerance, and time horizon to create a portfolio that's tailored to your unique needs. It's like having a custom-made suit, but for your money.
- **Automated Investing:** Say goodbye to manually buying and selling stocks. AI platforms can automatically execute trades for you, ensuring you never miss an opportunity. It's like having a personal

assistant who's always on top of your investments.

- **Lower Fees:** Traditional financial advisors often charge hefty fees, eating into your returns. AI platforms typically have much lower fees, or even no fees at all, so more of your money stays in your pocket.
- **24/7 Access:** Want to check on your investments at 2 AM? No problem! AI platforms are available anytime, anywhere, so you can stay on top of your finances even when you're on the go.
- **Educational Resources**: Many AI platforms offer educational resources, tutorials, and even virtual simulations to help you learn about investing and make informed decisions. It's like having a financial tutor in your back pocket.

**Real-World Example:**

Let's say you're a college student with a part-time job and some savings you want to invest. You sign up for an AI-powered investment platform and answer a few questions about your goals and risk tolerance. The platform then creates a diversified portfolio for you, automatically investing your money in a mix of stocks, bonds, and other assets. You can check on your investments anytime through the app, and the platform will even send you notifications about potential opportunities or risks. It's like having a financial advisor, but without the fancy office or the expensive fees.

**Strategies for Building a Diversified Portfolio**

Now, let's talk about one of the most important concepts in investing: diversification. It's like the old saying, "Don't put all your eggs in one basket." By spreading your investments across different asset classes, industries, and geographic regions, you reduce your risk and increase your chances of long-term success.

Think of it like building a superhero team. You wouldn't want a team of just Hulks, right? You need a mix of strengths and skills to tackle any challenge that comes your way. The same goes for your investment portfolio.

AI can be a powerful tool for building a diversified portfolio. It can analyze thousands of potential investments, identify those that fit your risk profile and goals, and even suggest optimal asset allocations. It's like having a financial strategist helping you assemble the perfect team of investments.

**Here are some key strategies for building a diversified portfolio with AI:**

- **Asset Allocation:** AI can help you determine the right mix of stocks, bonds, and other assets based on your risk tolerance and time horizon. For example, if you're young and have a long time horizon, you might want a more aggressive portfolio with a higher allocation to stocks. But if you're closer to retirement, you might want a more conservative portfolio with a higher allocation to bonds.
- **Industry Diversification:** Don't put all your money into one industry. AI can help you identify promising sectors and spread your

investments across different industries, reducing your exposure to any single company or sector.

- **Geographic Diversification:** The global economy is interconnected, but different regions can experience diffcrent growth patterns. AI can help you identify opportunities in emerging markets and diversify your portfolio across different countries.
- **Rebalancing:** Over time, the value of your investments will change, and your portfolio might become unbalanced. AI can automatically rebalance your portfolio, ensuring that your asset allocation stays in line with your goals.

## Real-World Example:

Let's say you're interested in sustainable investing. You want to invest in companies that are making a positive impact on the environment and society. AI can help you identify these companies and build a portfolio that aligns with your values. It can also track the performance of these companies and alert you to any potential risks or opportunities.

## AI Investing: Empowering Your Financial Future

AI investing isn't just about making money – it's about taking control of your financial future and building a life where you're empowered to pursue your dreams. It's about using technology to your advantage and creating a portfolio that reflects your values and aspirations.

Remember, the key is to start early, stay disciplined, and leverage the power of AI to make informed decisions. With the right tools and strategies, you can outsmart the market, supercharge your savings, and build a future where financial freedom is a reality.

## Chapter 5:

### Navigating the Risks and Rewards

Alright, my financially fearless Gen Z warriors, it's time for a reality check. Investing isn't all rainbows and unicorns. It's more like a rollercoaster ride, with thrilling ups and stomach-churning downs. But hey, that's part of the adventure, right?

In this chapter, we're going to dive headfirst into the wild world of market volatility and risk management. We'll talk about the importance of keeping your cool when the market throws a tantrum, and how AI can be your trusty sidekick, helping you stay focused on your long-term goals.

### Market Volatility: The Stock Market's Mood Swings

Let's face it, the stock market can be as unpredictable as a teenager's mood swings. One minute it's soaring to new heights, and the next, it's crashing down like a house of cards. It's enough to make even the most seasoned investors break out in a cold sweat.

But here's the thing: volatility is a natural part of the market. It's what makes investing exciting (and a little bit scary). Think of it like a thrilling amusement park ride - you wouldn't want it to be boring, would you?

**Real-World Example:**

Remember the GameStop saga of 2021? A group of Redditors banded together to drive up the price of GameStop stock, causing a massive short squeeze and sending Wall Street into a frenzy. The stock price went from under $20 to over $400 in a matter of weeks! But then, just as quickly as it rose, it came crashing back down.

That's volatility in action, folks. It's a wild ride, but it's also a reminder that the market can be unpredictable.

**Risk Management: Don't Put All Your Eggs in One Basket**

Now, I'm not saying you should avoid the stock market altogether. That would be like saying you should never go on a rollercoaster because it might be scary. But what I *am* saying is that you need to manage your risk.

Think of it like this: you wouldn't bet your entire life savings on a single hand of poker, would you? No way! You'd spread your bets, play it smart, and make sure you have enough chips left to keep playing the game.

The same principle applies to investing. You need to diversify your portfolio, spreading your investments across different asset classes, industries, and geographic regions. This way, if one investment takes a hit, others can help cushion the blow.

**Actionable Steps:**

- **Asset Allocation:** Decide on the right mix of stocks, bonds, and other assets based on your risk tolerance and time horizon. A good rule of thumb is to subtract your age from 100 to determine the percentage of your portfolio that should be invested in stocks. For example, if you're 25, you might want 75% of your portfolio in stocks and 25% in bonds.
- **Industry Diversification:** Don't put all your money into one industry, no matter how much you love it. Spread your investments across different sectors, like technology, healthcare, and consumer goods. This way, if one industry experiences a downturn, your entire portfolio won't be affected.
- **Geographic Diversification:** The world is your oyster! Don't limit yourself to just investing in your home country. Consider investing in international stocks or funds to tap into the growth potential of emerging markets.

**The Importance of Long-Term Investing: Slow and Steady Wins the Race**

Now, let's talk about one of the most important principles of investing: patience. Building wealth takes time. It's not about getting rich quick; it's about making smart decisions and letting your money grow steadily over the long term.

Think of it like planting a garden. You wouldn't expect to see a bountiful harvest overnight, would you? You need to nurture those seeds, water them regularly, and give them time to grow.

The same goes for your investments. Don't get discouraged if you don't see massive returns right away. Stay focused on your long-term goals, and let compound interest work its magic.

**Actionable Steps:**

- **Set realistic expectations:** Don't expect to become a millionaire overnight. Focus on building a solid foundation and making consistent contributions to your investments.
- **Avoid market timing:** Trying to time the market is like trying to catch lightning in a bottle. It's nearly impossible to predict short-term fluctuations. Instead, focus on long-term trends and invest consistently, regardless of market conditions.
- **Stay disciplined:** It's easy to get caught up in the excitement of a bull market or panic during a downturn. But remember, investing is a marathon, not a sprint. Stick to your plan and avoid making emotional decisions.

**Avoiding Emotional Decisions: Keep Your Cool When the Market Gets Hot (or Cold)**

Let's be honest, investing can be an emotional rollercoaster. When the market is soaring, it's easy to get caught up in the euphoria and make impulsive decisions. But when the market takes a nosedive, it's equally easy to panic and sell everything in a frenzy.

The key is to stay calm and avoid making decisions based on fear or greed. Remember, the market is always going to fluctuate. It's part of the game. But if you stick to your long-term plan and make rational decisions, you'll be well on your way to achieving your financial goals.

**Actionable Steps:**

- **Create an investment plan and stick to it:** Before you start investing, create a plan that outlines your goals, risk tolerance, and investment strategy. Review your plan regularly, but don't make drastic changes based on short-term market fluctuations.
- **Don't check your portfolio too often:** Constantly checking your investments can lead to anxiety and impulsive decisions. Instead, set a regular schedule for reviewing your portfolio, like once a quarter or once a year.
- **Talk to a financial advisor:** If you're feeling overwhelmed or unsure about your investments, don't hesitate to seek guidance from a financial advisor. They can help you create a plan, manage your risk, and stay on track to reach your goals.

**How AI Can Help You Stay Disciplined and Focused: Your Financial Fitness Coach**

Alright, Gen Z, let's talk about the real struggle when it comes to money: staying disciplined. It's easy to get caught up in the excitement of a hot new trend or panic when the market takes a dip. But let's be honest, investing isn't a sprint; it's a marathon. And just like any marathon, you need a coach to keep you motivated, focused, and on track.

That's where AI comes in. Think of it as your personal financial fitness coach, always there to cheer you on, push you harder, and help you reach your goals. AI can provide the structure, accountability, and personalized guidance you need to stay disciplined and make smart decisions, even when the going gets tough.

## Data-Driven Decision Making: Ditch the Emotional Rollercoaster

One of the biggest challenges in investing is managing your emotions. It's easy to get caught up in the hype and FOMO (fear of missing out) when the market is soaring. But when things take a downturn, it's equally easy to panic and make rash decisions that could derail your long-term goals. AI takes the emotion out of the equation. It analyzes data, not headlines. It looks at trends, not tweets. It helps you make decisions based on facts and logic, not fear and greed. Think of it like having a calm, rational voice in your ear, whispering, "Stay focused, you've got this!" even when the market is throwing a tantrum.

### Real-World Example:

Imagine you've invested in a company that's been on a hot streak. The stock price has doubled in the past few months, and everyone's talking about it. You're feeling pretty good about yourself, but then, out of nowhere, the company announces disappointing earnings, and the stock price plummets.

Your gut reaction might be to panic and sell, locking in your losses. But AI can help you see the bigger picture. It can analyze the company's fundamentals, compare it to its competitors, and assess the long-term outlook. Maybe this is just a temporary setback, and the company is still poised for growth. AI can help you make a rational decision based on data, not emotions.

**Personalized Goals and Progress Tracking: Your Financial Roadmap**

AI can also help you stay focused on your long-term goals by creating a personalized financial roadmap. It's like having a GPS for your money, guiding you every step of the way.

Think about it: when you're driving to a new destination, you wouldn't just hop in the car and start driving aimlessly, would you? No, you'd use a GPS to map out the best route, avoid traffic jams, and get you there efficiently.

AI investing platforms do the same thing for your finances. They help you set realistic goals, track your progress, and make adjustments as needed. It's like having a personal cheerleader, reminding you of your destination and celebrating your milestones along the way.

**Real-World Example:**

Let's say your goal is to save for a down payment on a house in five years. AI can help you break down that goal into smaller, more manageable steps. It can calculate how much you need to save each month, suggest investment strategies that align with your timeline, and even track your progress, so you can see how close you are to achieving your dream.

## Nudges and Reminders: Your Gentle (But Firm) Financial Coach

Let's face it, we all need a little nudge sometimes. Maybe it's a reminder to hit the gym, eat healthier, or, in this case, stick to your financial plan.

AI can be that gentle (but firm) financial coach, reminding you to stay on track and avoid impulsive decisions. It can send you notifications when it's time to rebalance your portfolio, make a contribution to your savings, or even just check in on your progress.

Think of it like having a workout buddy who texts you every morning to make sure you're getting out of bed and hitting the treadmill. It's that little extra push that can make all the difference in achieving your goals.

### Real-World Example:

You've been diligently saving for that dream vacation, but then a flash sale pops up for a pair of shoes you've been eyeing. You're tempted to splurge, but your AI-powered budgeting app sends you a notification reminding you of your savings goal. It's like having your own personal Jiminy Cricket, whispering in your ear, "Stay focused, stay focused!"

The Future of Financial Discipline: AI as Your Accountability Partner

AI is more than just a tool; it's a partner in your financial journey. It's there to support you, guide you, and help you stay disciplined, even when life throws you curveballs.

As AI technology continues to evolve, we can expect even more sophisticated tools and features that will empower you to take control of your financial future. Imagine AI-powered budgeting apps that learn your spending habits and automatically adjust your budget based on your lifestyle. Or, AI-driven investment platforms that use behavioral finance insights to help you avoid common investing mistakes.

The possibilities are endless, and the future of financial discipline is brighter than ever before. So, embrace the power of AI, let it be your accountability partner, and watch as your financial dreams become a reality.

**Actionable Steps:**

- **Set up alerts and notifications:** Use your AI platform to set up alerts and notifications that keep you informed about your investments. This will help you stay engaged and make timely decisions.
- **Utilize educational resources:** Many AI platforms offer educational resources and tutorials to help you learn about investing and make informed decisions. Take advantage of these resources to expand your knowledge and build your confidence.
- **Seek out community support:** Connect with other investors online or in person to share experiences, learn from each other, and stay motivated on your financial journey.

**Navigating the Risks and Rewards: You've Got This!**

Investing can be a wild ride, but with the right tools and mindset, you can navigate the ups and downs and achieve your financial goals. Remember, AI is your ally, providing you with the data, insights, and support you need to make informed decisions and stay on track.

**Chapter 6:**

**Hacking Your Habits with AI: Level Up Your Financial Game**

Alright, Gen Z, let's get real about our habits. We all have them - those little routines and patterns that shape our lives, for better or for worse. And when it comes to money, our habits can either be our biggest allies or our worst enemies. It's like that one friend who's always down for a spontaneous shopping spree or the other one who's constantly reminding you to save for a rainy day.

But here's the good news: we're not stuck with the habits we have. We can change them, upgrade them, and even hack them with a little help from our trusty sidekick, AI. Think of it as a financial glow-up, but instead of a new haircut and a killer outfit, we're talking about a mindset shift and some seriously smart tools to help you level up your financial game.

In this chapter, we're going to dive deep into the world of AI-powered habit hacking. We'll explore how AI can help you track your spending like a financial detective, set goals that actually stick (no more New Year's resolutions that fizzle out by February!), and automate your savings so you can build wealth on autopilot. Get ready to transform your financial life, one habit at a time!

## Track Your Spending: Unleash Your Inner Financial Detective

Let's face it, keeping track of every penny you spend can feel like a full-time job. Between subscription services, impulse buys, and those sneaky "small" expenses that add up over time, it's easy to lose sight of where your money is actually going. It's like trying to find a needle in a haystack, except the haystack is your bank statement and the needle is that $5 latte you swore you'd stop buying.

But fear not, my financially savvy friends, because AI is here to help you channel your inner Sherlock Holmes and crack the case of your spending habits.

AI-powered budgeting apps and tools can track your expenses automatically, categorizing them and giving you a clear picture of where your money is going. It's like having a personal financial detective working around the clock, analyzing your transactions and uncovering hidden spending patterns.

Think of it like this: you wouldn't go on a road trip without a map, would you? You need to know where you're starting from and where you're going. AI budgeting tools give you that financial map, showing you the twists and turns of your spending habits so you can navigate towards your goals.

**Real-World Example:**

Imagine you're a college student trying to balance your studies, social life, and a part-time job. You're constantly swiping your debit card, but you have no idea where all your money is going. You download a budgeting app like Mint, connect it to your bank accounts, and voila! Suddenly, you have a clear picture of your spending habits. You realize you're spending way more on takeout than you thought, and those "harmless" impulse buys at the campus bookstore are adding up.

Armed with this knowledge, you can make informed decisions about your spending. Maybe you start cooking more at home or set a monthly limit for discretionary spending. The point is, you're now in the driver's seat, not just blindly cruising along hoping for the best.

**Actionable Steps:**

1. Download a budgeting app: Choose an AI-powered budgeting app that connects to your bank accounts and credit cards. Some popular options include Mint, YNAB (You Need a Budget), and PocketGuard. Do some research, read reviews, and find one that fits your style and needs.
2. Set up automatic categorization: Most budgeting apps allow you to categorize your expenses automatically. But don't just set it

and forget it! Review these categorizations regularly to ensure they're accurate. You might be surprised to find that your morning coffee is being categorized as "groceries" instead of "dining out."

3. Set spending limits: Once you have a clear picture of your spending habits, it's time to set some boundaries. Think of it like creating a personal spending diet. Set realistic spending limits for each category, like groceries, entertainment, and transportation. This will help you stay on track and avoid those impulse buys that can derail your budget.

4. Review your spending regularly: Make it a habit to review your spending at least once a week. This will help you identify any areas where you might be slipping up and make adjustments as needed. It's like checking in with your financial coach to see how your training is going.

1. Utilize AI insights: Many budgeting apps offer AI-powered insights into your spending habits. These insights can help you identify trends, spot

potential savings opportunities, and even predict future expenses. It's like having a financial advisor in your pocket, whispering words of wisdom to help you make smarter choices.

**Set Financial Goals That Stick: Dream Big, Plan Smart**

Setting financial goals is like setting your GPS for a road trip. You need to know where you're going before you can start driving. But let's be honest, setting goals is easy; sticking to them is the hard part. It's like saying you're going to run a marathon, but then hitting the snooze button every morning instead of lacing up your sneakers.

That's where AI can be your ultimate accountability partner, your personal cheerleader, and your financial drill sergeant all rolled into one. AI-powered goal-setting tools can help you break down your big dreams into smaller, more manageable steps. They can also track your progress, provide personalized feedback, and even give you a virtual high-five when you reach a milestone.

Think of it like training for that marathon. You wouldn't just show up on race day and expect to win, would you? No, you'd create a training plan, track your mileage, and celebrate your progress along the way. AI goal-setting tools do the same thing for your finances, helping you stay motivated and focused on the finish line.

**Real-World Example:**

Let's say your dream is to buy your first home in five years. That's a big goal, and it can feel overwhelming, like climbing Mount Everest. But an AI-powered goal-setting tool can help you break it down into smaller, more manageable steps. It can calculate how much you need to save each month, suggest investment strategies to help you reach your target, and even track the housing market in your area to give you real-time updates. It's like having a Sherpa guide you up the mountain, one step at a time.

But AI doesn't just help you set goals; it also helps you stay motivated. It can send you reminders, offer encouragement, and even provide personalized tips and advice based on your progress. It's like having a personal cheerleader in your pocket, always reminding you of what you're working towards and celebrating your wins along the way.

**Actionable Steps:**

1. Identify your goals: What do you want to achieve with your money? Be specific and realistic. Instead of just saying "I want to be rich," try "I want to save $20,000 for a down payment on a house in five years." The more specific your goals, the easier it will be to create a plan and track your progress.
2. Break down your goals: Once you have your big goals, break them down into smaller, more

manageable steps. This will make them feel less daunting and more achievable. It's like tackling a big project by breaking it down into smaller tasks - suddenly, it doesn't seem so overwhelming.

3. Use AI-powered goal-setting tools: There are many great AI-powered tools that can help you set, track, and achieve your financial goals. Some popular options include Digit, Qapital, and Clarity Money. These tools can automate your savings, track your progress, and even give you personalized recommendations based on your spending habits.

4. Visualize your success: Create a vision board or write down your goals where you can see them every day. This will help you stay motivated and focused on what you're working towards. It's like having a constant reminder of your dreams, pushing you to keep going even when things get tough.

1. Celebrate your progress: Don't wait until you reach the finish line to celebrate. Acknowledge your small wins along the way. Did you stick to your budget for a whole month?

High-five! Did you reach a savings milestone? Treat yourself to something special (within reason, of course!). Celebrating your progress will keep you motivated and excited about your financial journey.

**Automate Your Savings: Build Wealth on Autopilot**

Let's be honest, saving money can be tough. There's always something tempting to spend your hard-earned cash on – a new outfit, a night out with friends, or the latest gadget. But what if you could save money without even thinking about it?

That's the beauty of automation. By setting up automatic transfers and using AI-powered savings tools, you can build wealth on autopilot. It's like having a personal savings robot working tirelessly behind the scenes, putting money away for you even when you're tempted to splurge.

Think of it like this: you wouldn't manually brush your teeth every time you eat, would you? No, you'd use an electric toothbrush that does the work for you. Automation is all about making your life easier and freeing up your mental energy for more important things.

**Real-World Example:**

Imagine you're a recent college grad, working your first full-time job and finally making some decent money. You're excited about your newfound financial independence, but you also know you need to start saving for the future. The problem is, life is expensive! There's rent, student loan payments, groceries, transportation, and let's not forget those weekend brunches and concert tickets.

It feels like there's never enough money left over to save. But then, you discover the power of automation. You set up an automatic transfer of $100 from your paycheck to your savings account every month. It's not a huge amount, but it's a start.

You also download an AI-powered savings app like Acorns. Every time you make a purchase with your debit card, Acorns rounds up the transaction to the nearest dollar and invests the spare change for you. It's like saving money without even realizing it!

A few months go by, and you check your savings account. To your surprise, you've already saved over $1,000! And your Acorns account is starting to grow, too. You realize that automation is a game-changer. It's taken the stress and effort out of saving, allowing you to build wealth effortlessly.

Now, you're not just dreaming about your financial goals; you're actively working towards them. You're building a solid foundation for your future, one automatic transfer and rounded-up purchase at a time.

**Actionable Steps:**

Set up automatic transfers: The easiest way to save money is to make it automatic. Set up a recurring transfer from your checking account to your savings account each month. Start small and gradually increase the amount as you can.

Use AI-powered savings tools: There are many AI-powered tools that can help you save more money effortlessly. Some popular options include Acorns, Chime, and Digit. These tools can automate your savings, track your progress, and even give you personalized recommendations based on your spending habits.

Take advantage of employer matching programs: If your employer offers a 401(k) or other retirement savings plan with matching contributions, take advantage of it! It's free money, people! Don't leave that on the table. Make saving fun: Set up challenges or rewards for yourself to make saving more enjoyable. For example, you could challenge yourself to save $100 a month for six months and then treat yourself to a weekend getaway or a new gadget.

**Hack Your Habits, Transform Your Life**

Remember, your habits shape your reality. By hacking your financial habits with the power of AI, you can transform your relationship with money and create a life of abundance and freedom. It's time to ditch the old patterns that are holding you back and embrace new, empowering habits that will propel you towards your dreams.

So, what are you waiting for? Download those budgeting apps, set those financial goals, and automate your savings. Let AI be your guide on this exciting journey to financial wellness. You've got this!

**Chapter 7:**

**The Future is Yours: Building Wealth on Your Terms**

Alright, my Gen Z go-getters, we've laid the groundwork, busted some myths, and even hacked a few habits. Now, it's time to unleash your inner financial badass and build the kind of wealth that sets you free to live life on *your* terms.

This chapter is your mini-financial masterclass, packed with real-world examples, actionable steps, and a whole lot of inspiration. We're going to show you how AI can be your ultimate wealth-building tool, helping you make smarter investment decisions, maximize your returns, and create a future where financial worries are a distant memory. Get ready to level up your money game and step into a world of possibilities!

**AI-Powered Investing: Your Secret Weapon for Outsmarting the Market**

Remember that feeling when you finally beat that impossible level in your favorite video game? It's a rush, right? Well, AI investing can give you that same feeling of triumph, but instead of virtual coins, you're racking up real-world wealth.

AI-powered investment platforms aren't just about automating your finances; they're about giving you an edge, a secret weapon to outsmart the market and achieve your financial goals faster. Let's explore some of the ways AI can help you become a financial ninja:

1. **Data-Driven Insights:** AI algorithms can analyze massive amounts of data in real-time, identifying trends, patterns, and potential investment opportunities that humans might miss. It's like having a team of financial analysts working around the clock, crunching numbers and uncovering hidden gems.

**Real-World Example**:

Imagine you're passionate about saving the planet and want your investments to reflect that. You're interested in putting your money into renewable energy companies, but let's be honest, researching every single company out there would take forever! This is where AI swoops in like your eco-conscious financial superhero. It can leverage a combination of powerful technologies to help you build a green and profitable portfolio:

**Natural Language Processing (NLP):** AI with NLP capabilities can scan through tons of news articles, company reports, and even social media chatter to identify companies actively involved in renewable energy. It can spot keywords like "solar," "wind," "sustainability," and "green initiatives" to create a shortlist of potential investments.

**Machine Learning:** Once you have a list of companies, AI can dig deeper, using machine learning algorithms to analyze their financial performance, growth potential, and overall market trends. It's like having a team of financial analysts working 24/7 to crunch the numbers and give you the insights you need.

**Big Data Analysis:** AI can also tap into vast datasets, including satellite imagery, to assess the real-world impact of renewable energy companies. For example, it can analyze the growth of solar panel installations or the efficiency of wind farms to identify companies that are truly making a difference.

**Sentiment Analysis:** Social media isn't just for memes and cat videos. AI can analyze social media sentiment to gauge public opinion and identify companies that are gaining traction and positive buzz in the renewable energy space. It's like having a finger on the pulse of the market, helping you spot trends before they become mainstream.

**How You Can Get These Results:**

**Choose an AI-Powered Investment Platform:** Look for platforms that specialize in sustainable or ESG (Environmental, Social, and Governance) investing. These platforms often use AI to identify and evaluate companies based on their environmental impact, social responsibility, and corporate governance practices.

**Set Your Preferences:** Most AI platforms allow you to customize your investment preferences. You can specify your desired level of exposure to renewable energy companies, your risk tolerance, and your investment goals.

**1. How AI Can Manage Your Portfolio:**

**Let AI Do the Heavy Lifting:** Once you've set your preferences, sit back and let AI do its magic. The platform will use its algorithms to create a personalized portfolio of renewable energy investments that align with your values and financial goals.

**Monitor and Adjust:** Regularly review your portfolio's performance and make adjustments as needed. AI can provide ongoing insights and recommendations, but it's important to stay informed and engaged in the process.

By leveraging the power of AI, you can build a green portfolio that not only aligns with your values but also has the potential to generate strong returns. It's a win-win for you and the planet!

1. **Risk Management and Diversification:** We've already talked about the importance of diversification, but AI takes it to a whole new level. It can help you build a portfolio that's perfectly balanced for your risk tolerance and goals, ensuring you're not putting all your eggs in one basket. It's like having a financial advisor who's constantly monitoring your investments and making adjustments to keep you on track.

**Real-World Example:**

Let's say you're a young investor with a thirst for adventure and a high-risk tolerance. You're not afraid to take a chance on the next big thing, even if it means weathering some ups and downs along the way. You're dreaming of those high-growth potential stocks, the ones that could turn a small investment into a fortune.

But here's the thing: even the most seasoned investors know that chasing high-growth stocks can be a risky game. It's like riding a rollercoaster – exhilarating, but also potentially nausea-inducing. That's where AI comes in, acting as your financial safety net.

**How AI Does It:**

**Predictive Analytics:** AI algorithms can analyze vast amounts of historical market data, company financials, and even news sentiment to identify stocks with high-growth potential. It's like having a team of financial analysts working around the clock, crunching numbers and spotting trends that might indicate a company is poised for a breakout.

**Risk Assessment:** While AI can help you identify potential winners, it also understands the importance of risk management. It can assess the volatility and potential downside of high-growth stocks, ensuring that you're not putting all your eggs in one basket. It's like having a financial guardian angel, reminding you to diversify your portfolio and protect your hard-earned money.

**Portfolio Optimization:** AI can help you create a balanced portfolio that aligns with your risk tolerance and goals. It can suggest a mix of high-growth stocks, along with safer investments like bonds or index funds, to create a diversified portfolio that can weather market storms. It's like having a personal financial coach, helping you build a strong and resilient investment strategy.

**Real-Time Monitoring and Alerts:** AI can keep a constant eye on your investments, alerting you to any significant changes or potential risks. This allows you to make informed decisions and adjust your portfolio as needed, even in a fast-moving market. It's like having a financial watchdog, barking whenever something needs your attention.

**What You Need to Do:**

**Choose an AI-Powered Platform with Risk Assessment Tools:** Look for platforms that offer advanced risk assessment and portfolio optimization features. These tools will help you identify high-growth potential stocks while ensuring that your overall portfolio remains balanced and aligned with your risk tolerance.

**Set Clear Investment Goals:** Define your financial goals and time horizon. Are you saving for a down payment on a house in five years, or are you looking to build long-term wealth for retirement? This will help AI tailor its recommendations to your specific needs.

**Be Honest About Your Risk Tolerance:** AI can help you manage risk, but it's important to be honest with yourself and the platform about how much risk you're comfortable with. Don't let the allure of high returns tempt you into taking on more risk than you can handle.

**Review and Adjust Regularly:** The market is constantly changing, so it's important to review your portfolio regularly and make adjustments as needed. AI can help you stay on top of things, but it's still your responsibility to make informed decisions.

1. ## Personalized Recommendations: AI can take into account your individual circumstances, goals, and risk tolerance to provide personalized investment recommendations. It's like having a financial advisor who knows you inside and out, tailoring their advice to your specific needs. No more generic investment strategies that don't fit your lifestyle or aspirations.

**Real-World Example:**

Picture this: you're fresh out of college, diploma in hand, but also saddled with a hefty pile of student loan debt. It's like a dark cloud hanging over your head, making it hard to even think about saving or investing for the future. But you've got big dreams – you want to start your own business, be your own boss, and create something amazing. This is where AI steps in, not just as a financial advisor, but as a strategic partner in your journey to entrepreneurship.

**How AI Does It:**

**Goal Prioritization and Planning:** AI-powered financial planning tools can help you create a personalized roadmap that balances your short-term needs (like paying down debt) with your long-term goals (like saving for your business). It's like having a financial GPS that calculates the best route to reach your destination, taking into account all the obstacles and detours along the way.

**Cash Flow Optimization:** AI can analyze your income and expenses to identify areas where you can cut back and free up more cash flow to put towards your debt and savings goals. It's like having a financial detective, sniffing out those sneaky expenses that are draining your bank account.

**Investment Strategy Tailored to Your Goals:** AI can recommend investment strategies that align with your risk tolerance and time horizon, ensuring that you're making the most of your money while still prioritizing debt repayment. It's like having a personal investment coach, cheering you on and helping you make smart choices every step of the way.

**Automated Savings and Debt Payments:** AI can automate your savings and debt payments, making it easier to stay on track and avoid missed payments or late fees. It's like having a financial assistant who takes care of the boring stuff so you can focus on building your business.

By leveraging the power of AI, you can create a financial plan that's as unique as you are. It's not about sacrificing your dreams or delaying your goals; it's about finding the right balance and using technology to your advantage. With AI as your financial wingman, you can conquer your student loan debt and launch your business with confidence.

## Real-World Example: Tax Season Doesn't Have to Be a Nightmare

Okay, let's talk about something that's about as fun as a root canal: taxes. They can be a major drag on your investment returns, eating into your hard-earned profits. But fear not, my financially savvy friends, because AI is here to save the day (and your money!).

### How AI Does It:

**Tax-Efficient Investment Strategies:** AI-powered platforms can help you identify investment strategies that minimize your tax burden. This might include investing in tax-advantaged accounts like IRAs or 401(k)s, or choosing investments that generate long-term capital gains, which are taxed at a lower rate than short-term gains.It's like having a tax-savvy advisor whispering in your ear, "Hey, this investment will save you a bundle on taxes!"

**Tax-Loss Harvesting:** This fancy-sounding term basically means selling investments that have lost value to offset capital gains taxes. It's a smart strategy, but it can be tricky to implement manually. AI can automate this process, identifying opportunities to harvest losses and maximize your tax savings. It's like having a tax ninja slicing and dicing your portfolio to minimize your tax bill.

**Navigating Complex Tax Regulations:** Tax laws can be as confusing as a choose-your-own-adventure book, but AI can help you navigate the maze. It can keep track of changing regulations, identify potential deductions and credits, and even flag potential red flags that could trigger an audit. It's like having a tax expert on speed dial, ready to answer your questions and keep you on the right side of the IRS. AI can turn tax season from a dreaded chore into a strategic opportunity. You can minimize your tax burden, keep more of your hard-earned money, and focus on what really matters - building your financial future.

So, there you have it – two real-world examples of how AI can be your financial wingman, helping you achieve your goals and overcome challenges. Remember, AI is a powerful tool, but it's up to you to wield it wisely. So, embrace the technology, stay informed, and let AI help you build the life you deserve.

**Real-World Example:**

You've made some profitable investments, but you're worried about the tax implications. AI can analyze your portfolio and suggest strategies to minimize your tax liability, such as selling certain investments at a loss to offset your gains. It's like having a tax ninja fighting for every penny you deserve.

**Actionable Steps:**

1. **Choose the Right AI Platform:** Do your research and find an AI-powered investment platform that aligns with your needs and goals. Look for platforms that offer personalized portfolios, automated investing, low fees, educational resources, and strong customer support. Some popular options

include Wealthfront, Betterment, and M1 Finance.

2. **Set Clear Financial Goals:** What do you want to achieve with your money? Do you want to buy a house, travel the world, or retire early? The more specific your goals, the easier it will be for AI to create a personalized investment plan for you.

3. **Be Honest About Your Risk Tolerance:** How much risk are you comfortable with? Are you willing to ride the ups and downs of the market for the potential of higher returns, or do you prefer a more conservative approach? Be honest with yourself and your AI platform so it can create a portfolio that matches your risk appetite.

4. **Monitor Your Progress Regularly:** Don't just set it and forget it. Check in on your investments regularly to see how they're performing and make adjustments as needed. AI can help you track your progress and provide insights into your portfolio's performance, but it's still important to stay engaged and informed.

1. **Don't Be Afraid to Ask for Help:**
   If you have questions or concerns
   about your investments, don't
   hesitate to reach out to the customer
   support team of your AI platform or
   consult with a financial advisor.
   Remember, you're not alone on this
   journey. The future of finance is in
   your hands. You have the power to
   break free from the traditional mold,
   challenge the status quo, and create
   a life where you're in control of your
   financial destiny.

**Chapter 8:**

**Conclusion: Your Financial Adventure Awaits!**

Alright, my Gen Z financial rockstars, we've reached
the end of our journey together. We've laughed,
we've learned, and we've hopefully inspired you to
take control of your financial destiny. But before we
say our goodbyes, let's recap some of the key
takeaways and leave you with a sense of
empowerment and excitement for the incredible
financial adventure that awaits.

**Key Takeaways: Your AI-Powered Financial
Toolkit**

Throughout this book, we've explored the amazing
ways AI can supercharge your savings and help you
build a brighter financial future. Let's recap some of
the most important lessons we've learned:

- **AI is your financial wingman:** It's not just a buzzword or a futuristic concept; it's a powerful tool that can help you make smarter decisions, achieve your goals faster, and build wealth on your terms.

- **Embrace technology:** Don't be afraid to leverage the latest AI-powered tools and platforms to manage your finances. They're designed to be user-friendly, accessible, and affordable.

- **Start early and stay consistent:** The earlier you start saving and investing, the more time your money has to grow. Even small contributions, made regularly, can lead to significant wealth over time thanks to the magic of compound interest.

- **Diversification is key:** Don't put all your eggs in one basket. Spread your investments across different asset classes, industries, and geographic regions to reduce risk and maximize your potential for returns.

- **Stay disciplined and avoid emotional decisions:** The market will have its ups and downs, but don't let fear or greed dictate your investment choices. Stick to your plan and make rational decisions based on data, not emotions.

- **AI can help you hack your habits:** From tracking your spending to setting goals to automating your savings, AI can help you develop healthier financial habits and stay on track.

- **The future is yours:** You have the power to create the financial future you desire. Embrace innovation, leverage technology, and never stop learning.

**Real-World Examples: AI in Action**

Let's revisit some of the real-world examples we've explored throughout this book and see how AI is already making a difference in the lives of young investors:

- Sarah, a college student with a passion for sustainability, used an AI-powered investment platform to build a portfolio focused on renewable energy companies. She's now not only contributing to a greener future but also seeing her investments grow steadily.
- David, a recent graduate with student loan debt, leveraged AI-powered budgeting and goal-setting tools to create a personalized financial plan. He's now on track to pay off his debt and save for a down payment on his first home.
- Maria, a young entrepreneur, used AI to analyze market trends and identify a gap in the market for her new product. She's now running a successful business and building a secure financial future.

**How AI Makes it Happen:**

- Sarah's AI platform utilized Natural Language Processing (NLP) to scan news articles and social media for mentions of renewable energy companies, and machine learning algorithms to analyze their financial performance and growth potential.

- David's budgeting app used AI to track his spending habits and identify areas where he could cut back. His goal-setting tool used AI to calculate his savings targets and suggest investment strategies based on his timeline and risk tolerance.
- Maria's AI-powered market research tool analyzed consumer behavior, social media trends, and competitor data to identify a niche market for her product.

**Actionable Steps: Your Financial Adventure Starts Now!**

It's time to take the knowledge you've gained from this book and put it into action. Here are some concrete steps you can take today to start building your financial future:

1. **Assess your financial situation:** Take a good, hard look at your income, expenses, debts, and savings. Be honest with yourself about where you stand financially.
2. **Set clear financial goals:** What do you want to achieve with your money? Be specific and realistic, and break down your big goals into smaller, more manageable steps.
3. **Create a budget:** Use AI-powered budgeting tools to track your

spending, set limits, and identify areas where you can save more.

4. **Start investing:** Even if you can only invest a small amount, start now. Choose an AI-powered investment platform that aligns with your goals and risk tolerance.

5. **Automate your savings:** Set up automatic transfers to your savings and investment accounts so you can build wealth on autopilot.

6. **Stay informed and educated:** Continue learning about investing and personal finance. Read books, listen to podcasts, and follow experts in the field.

7. **Seek out community and support:** Connect with other young investors online or in person to share experiences, learn from each other, and stay motivated.

8. **Embrace the power of AI:** Don't be afraid to experiment with different AI-powered tools and platforms. Find the ones that work best for you and leverage their capabilities to achieve your financial goals.

**Resources for Further Exploration**

- **Books:**
  - "The Automatic Millionaire" by David Bach
  - "Broke Millennial" by Erin Lowry
  - "The Psychology of Money" by Morgan Housel
- **Podcasts:**
  - "So Money" with Farnoosh Torabi
  - "The Dave Ramsey Show"
  - "ChooseFI"
- **Websites and Apps:**
  - NerdWallet
  - Investopedia
  - Robinhood
  - Acorns
  - Betterment

**Your Financial Future is Bright!**

Gen Z, you're not just the future; you're a force of nature, a generation bursting with creativity, passion, and a hunger to make a difference. You have the power to reshape the world, and that includes the world of finance. With AI as your ally, you're not just building a secure financial future; you're crafting a life of limitless possibilities.

Imagine waking up each day with the freedom to pursue your passions, the confidence to chase your wildest dreams, and the resources to make a real impact on the world. That's the power of financial empowerment, and it's within your reach.

So, go out there and unleash your full potential! Start that business you've been dreaming about, travel the world and experience different cultures, give back to your community and make a positive difference. The only limits are the ones you set for yourself.

Remember, you're not alone on this journey. We're all in this together, cheering you on and celebrating your successes.There are countless resources, tools, and communities available to support you every step of the way. So, keep learning, keep growing, and never let anyone tell you that your dreams are too big.

The future is yours. It's bright, it's bold, and it's waiting for you to grab it with both hands. Go out there and make it happen! The world is ready for you.

## References

- Bach, D. (2004). *The Automatic Millionaire.* Broadway Books.
- Housel, M. (2020). *The Psychology of Money: Timeless lessons on wealth, greed, and happiness.* Harriman House.
- Lowry, E. (2017). *Broke Millennial: Stop scraping by and get your financial life together.* TarcherPerigee.
- Robbins, M. (2021). *The High 5 Habit: Take Control of Your Life with One Simple Habit.* Hay House, Inc.

## Websites and Apps

- Acorns. (n.d.). https://www.acorns.com/
- Betterment. (n.d.). https://www.betterment.com/
- Chime. (n.d.). https://www.chime.com/

- Digit. (n.d.). https://digit.co/
- Fidelity Renewable Energy Fund. (n.d.). [invalid URL removed]
- Investopedia. (n.d.). https://www.investopedia.com/
- M1 Finance. (n.d.). https://m1finance.com/
- Mint. (n.d.). https://www.mint.com/
- NerdWallet. (n.d.). https://www.nerdwallet.com/
- PocketGuard. (n.d.). https://pocketguard.com/
- Qapital. (n.d.). https://www.qapital.com/
- QQQ. (n.d.). https://www.invesco.com/qqq-etf/en/home.html
- Robinhood. (n.d.). https://robinhood.com/
- Wealthfront. (n.d.). https://www.wealthfront.com/
- YNAB (You Need a Budget). (n.d.). https://www.youneedabudget.com/

**Note:** Please ensure to verify and update the URLs and publication details as needed, as websites and app information may change over time.

**Disclaimer:** This book is intended for informational purposes only and does not constitute financial advice. Please consult with a qualified financial advisor before making any investment decisions.